SALLY RIDE
AND THE SHUTTLE MISSIONS

Andrew Langley

heinemann
raintree

© 2016 Heinemann-Raintree
an imprint of Capstone Global Library, LLC
Chicago, Illinois

To contact Capstone Global Library please call 800-747-4992, or visit our web site
www.capstonepub.com

Edited by Clare Lewis and Abby Colich
Designed by Steve Mead and Justin Hoffman
Original illustrations © Capstone Global Library Ltd. 2015
Illustrated by Justin Hoffman
Picture research by Svetlana Zhurkin
Production by Victoria Fitzgerald
Originated by Capstone Global Library Ltd.

Library of Congress Cataloging-in-Publication Data
Langley, Andrew, 1949- author.

 Sally Ride and the shuttle missions / Andrew Langley.
   pages cm.—(Adventures in space)
 Includes bibliographical references and index.
 ISBN 978-1-4846-2516-3 (hb)—ISBN 978-1-4846-2521-7 (pb)—ISBN 978-1-4846-2531-6 (ebook) 1.
Ride, Sally—Juvenile literature. 2. Women astronauts—United States—Biography—Juvenile literature.
3. Astronauts—United States—Biography—Juvenile literature. 4. Space shuttles—Juvenile literature. 5.
Manned space flight—Juvenile literature. 6. Outer space—Exploration—Juvenile literature. I. Title.
 TL789.85.R53L36 2016
 629.450092—dc23   2015000267
 [B]

This book has been officially leveled using the F&P Text Level Gradient™ Levelling System.

Acknowledgments
We would like to thank the following for permission to reproduce photographs:
AP Photo, 31, Dave Pickoff, 33; Getty Images: Archive Photos/Robert Alexander, 18, Space Frontiers,
17; NASA, cover (top, bottom right), 4, 5, 11, 12, 13, 14, 20, 21, 23, 24, 26, 27, 28, 29, 32, 34, 37
(front), 41, Bill Ingalls, 39, ESA/Hubble SM4 ERO Team, 37 (back), Kennedy Space Center, 42, NOAA/
GSFC/Suomi NPP/VIIRS/Norman Kuring, 30; Newscom: NASA, 43, TASS/Albert Pushkarev, 40, Zuma
Press/Kommersant/Ogonyok, 7, Zuma Press/Pamela Price, 35; Shutterstock: 3Dsculptor, cover (bottom
left); Stanford News Service: Chuck Painter, 9

We would like to thank Dr. Geza Gyuk for his invaluable help in the preparation of this book.

CONTENTS

All words in bold, **like this**, appear in the glossary on page 45.

INTO SPACE

Sally Ride was going up—in an elevator. Higher and higher it went, nearly 147 feet (45 meters) in the air. Ride and the four other **astronauts** got out. They climbed through a **hatch** into the cabin of the white space shuttle. They were strapped into their seats. In under two hours, they would be launched into space.

LIFTOFF

The space shuttle was standing on its tail on the launchpad. It was fixed to something even bigger—a giant fuel tank. On either side were two white rockets. Ride and the crew members checked their controls and waited.

The shuttle was attached to a huge tank, which contained enough fuel to carry it into space.

SPACE SPEAK

Rocket boosters: The two rockets provide most of the launch power, zooming the shuttle up to 30 miles (45 kilometers) in two minutes and boosting it to a speed of almost 3,000 miles (5,000 kilometers) per hour. Then they separate from the fuel tank and fall back into the sea. The rockets can be cleaned out and re-used.

The countdown began: ten...nine...eight. At seven, the shuttle's engine started. At one, the **rocket boosters** roared into life and the craft began to lift away from the ground. Suddenly, the astronauts were hurtling through the clouds. The rockets burned out and fell away, but the shuttle carried on out of Earth's **atmosphere**.

THE FIRST AMERICAN WOMAN IN SPACE

On June 18, 1983, Sally Ride became the first American woman to go into space. She was also the youngest-ever astronaut. Her flight was on board the shuttle *Challenger*, launched from the Kennedy Space Center in Florida. She went on to make a second shuttle flight before becoming a college professor and author. She is one of the most famous people in the history of space travel.

The mission patch on Sally Ride's shirt commemorated her historic flight in *Challenger*.

A TALENTED GIRL

Sally Ride was born in Los Angeles, California, on May 26, 1951. She grew up to be a bright and determined teenager who was gifted at math and science. She was also a natural athlete and became an outstanding tennis player.

A LANDMARK FOR WOMEN

When Sally was just 12, in 1963, the very first woman went into space. She wasn't American, but Russian. Her name was Valentina Tereshkova, and she was a factory worker whose only experience of flying was with her local parachuting club.

Tereshkova was one of several women selected to train as cosmonauts (the Russian name for "astronauts"). After only 15 months of training, she was chosen to be the first woman in space. On June 16, 1963, she took off aboard the spacecraft *Vostok 6*. After nearly three days and 48 **orbits** of Earth, she parachuted safely back to land.

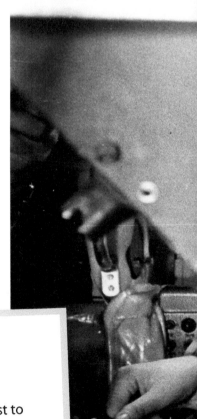

The Space Race

After World War II ended in 1945, the United States and Russia competed in many areas, including the exploration of space. This struggle became known as the Space Race. The Russians were first to launch a **satellite** (in 1957) and to launch a man into space (in 1961). But the United States was the first to land people on the Moon (in 1969).

FIRST TO THE MOON

Like many young people in the 1960s, Ride was thrilled by the race into space. Later, she watched the live TV footage of the first Moon landing in 1969. But she had no dreams of going into space herself, because astronauts were mostly men. "I just assumed there would never be a place for women," she said.

Valentina Tereshkova was 26 years old when she became the first woman in space.

THE UNITED STATES FALLS BEHIND

The Russians had chosen a female cosmonaut, but things were very different in the United States. At the time, women couldn't be selected to become astronauts. All sorts of reasons were given, including that women weren't strong enough for space travel or they might upset male astronauts.

Instead, Ride worked hard at her education. In 1970, she went to Stanford University, in California, where, besides her tennis triumphs, she gained degrees in English and **physics**. Her main subject was astronomy—the study of objects in space. She enjoyed college life and decided to apply for a teaching job after she graduated.

A CAREER IN SPACE

Then, in January 1977, Ride saw a headline in the local Stanford newspaper: "NASA to Recruit Women." NASA (the U.S. National Aeronautics and Space Administration) was openly advertising for female candidates. For the first time, women would be accepted for astronaut training.

She immediately wrote to apply. There was a long wait. More than 8,000 others had applied, too, and they all had to go through a series of tests and interviews. At last, a year later, Ride was told she'd made it.

Mercury 13

Mercury 13 is the name given to 13 American women who trained to become astronauts in the United States in the early 1960s. At the time, the United States was planning to put its first astronaut into space. The women underwent grueling tests to become part of the space team known as the First Lady Astronaut Trainees (FLAT). Despite the fact that the women performed exceptionally well, the FLAT project was not led by NASA, and it was abandoned. The 13 women never made it into space. However, their determination and dedication paved the way for future female astronauts.

Passing the test

These are some of the tests Sally Ride had to take before being selected for NASA:

- running on a treadmill to check that her heart was in good condition

- being zipped into a pitch-black chamber, to see how she reacted to the dark

- interviewing with **psychiatrists**, who assessed her personality

- writing an essay on why she wanted to go into space.

The radio telescope "Dish" (used for observing the stars) was at the center of Sally Ride's studies at Stanford University.

TRAINING TO BE AN ASTRONAUT

When Sally Ride joined the astronaut program, NASA was launching a brand-new project. Instead of heading for the Moon, it planned to focus on the area of space closer to Earth, known as **Low Earth Orbit**. There were space stations and satellites here already, which needed to be supplied and maintained.

A NEW KIND OF JOB

So, the job of an astronaut was changing. Space crew members had always been skilled air pilots, with a lot of experience flying jet aircraft. Now, NASA was also looking for people with different skills. Engineers were needed to build and repair spacecraft. Scientists were needed to carry out experiments and collect data in space. These new types of astronauts were called mission specialists.

SPACE SPEAK

Low Earth Orbit: Low Earth Orbit isn't very far away—it is between about 100 and 1,240 miles (160 and 2,000 kilometers) from Earth. If you drove a car straight upward, you'd reach it in around three hours. The Moon is a lot farther—it's an average of 237,700 miles (382,500 kilometers) away from Earth, and it would take you more than four months of nonstop driving to get there!

SPECIALIST, AND FEMALE

Ride was chosen to be a mission specialist because she was a highly qualified scientist. In addition to having advanced degrees in physics, she had done research into the gases that surround stars.

She was one of only six women among 35 new NASA recruits. This wasn't easy. The first female astronauts caused a massive wave of interest from the media and became famous overnight. They also had to live with hostility from some of the male astronauts, who were not used to working with women.

Ride (fourth from left) was one of six women astronaut trainees. All of them made flights into space.

LEARNING TO FLY

Ride faced a year of training at the Johnson Space Center in Houston, Texas, before she became an astronaut. Here she spent long days in the classroom, learning about everything from the oceans and rocks to the space shuttle engine.

Trainee mission specialists had to get used to air travel, so Ride spent many hours in jet trainer aircraft. After learning to navigate and operate the other instruments, she was trained to fly and land the aircraft herself. Her teachers were amazed by how quickly she became an expert pilot.

She also learned to operate another kind of machine. This was the robot arm—a crane fixed to the shuttle that was used to lift equipment and grab satellites out of the sky. Ride was soon the best arm operator in her class.

The astronauts learned to fly the shuttle by using a life-sized model of the real thing.

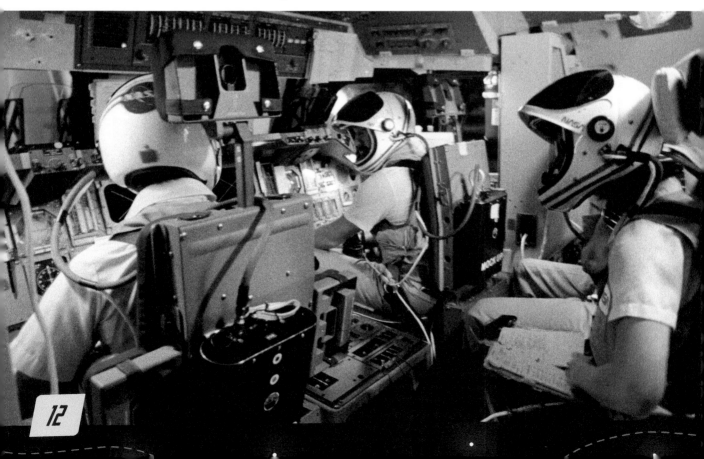

Here, Ride is taking part in a mission sequence test as part of her training.

ON A MISSION

On April 19, 1982, Ride got the best news of her life. She had been chosen for the next shuttle mission. Once again, her career was front-page news, and she appeared at a **press conference** to answer questions about her selection as the first American woman in space.

There was now a full year of special preparation for the flight. The crew members practiced every move of the journey many times, working in full-sized models of the shuttle. They prepared for any emergency— even for one of them being killed.

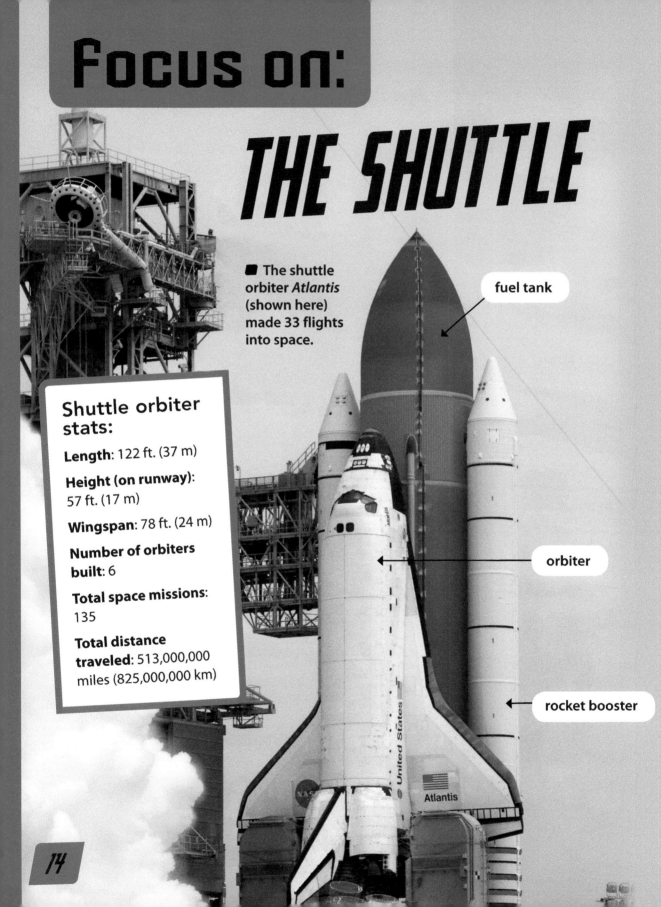

Focus on:

THE SHUTTLE

■ The shuttle orbiter *Atlantis* (shown here) made 33 flights into space.

fuel tank

orbiter

rocket booster

Shuttle orbiter stats:

Length: 122 ft. (37 m)

Height (on runway): 57 ft. (17 m)

Wingspan: 78 ft. (24 m)

Number of orbiters built: 6

Total space missions: 135

Total distance traveled: 513,000,000 miles (825,000,000 km)

The first space shuttle was launched into space from Florida on April 12, 1981. This was a new kind of craft, made specially to work in Low Earth Orbit. It was also planned to be much cheaper than previous spacecraft.

USED AGAIN AND AGAIN

What would make it cheaper? Each shuttle could be used many times. Parts of previous craft were designed to burn away upon re-entry into Earth's atmosphere. Large parts of earlier rockets were also thrown away on the way up to orbit. As a result, rockets could only fly once. But a shuttle was mostly kept intact during its journey. It was barely damaged and could be refurbished and re-used. Most of the shuttle fleet kept flying for 30 years, until it was retired in 2011.

WHAT WAS THE SPACE SHUTTLE FOR?

- It carried satellites into space and sent them into orbit around Earth.
- It transported large parts into space to help build the International Space Station.
- It repaired and maintained satellites and space stations.
- It took astronauts to space stations and back.
- It was a science laboratory where research was carried out in space.

Parts of the shuttle system

The orbiter

The orbiter looked like a small airliner, with a cabin at the front for the crew. On the descent to Earth, its engines were stopped. It came in to land like a **glider**.

The fuel tank

The giant tank contained a mixture of oxygen and hydrogen. This fuel powered the orbiter's engines.

The rocket boosters

The two rockets shot the orbiter to speeds of 5 miles (8 kilometers) per second, enough to put it into orbit.

SPACE Q AND A

Q. How did astronauts learn to fly the shuttle?

A. Ride and the crew learned to fly on simulators. These are computer screens that show an electronic imitation of the real thing.

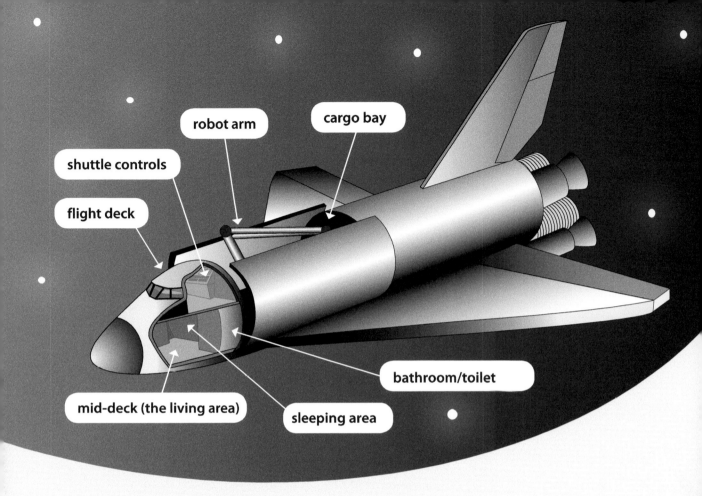

robot arm

cargo bay

shuttle controls

flight deck

bathroom/toilet

mid-deck (the living area)

sleeping area

INSIDE A SPACE SHUTTLE

At the front of the craft is the flight deck. Most of the controls are here, with seats for the pilot and commander. Beneath it is the mid deck, where the crew eats, sleeps, and works. The biggest part of the shuttle is the cargo bay at the back. This carries satellites and other equipment, as well as the robot arm. The crew can get into the cargo bay through the **air lock**.

CHALLENGER

Sally Ride's first flight was number STS-7. This meant it was the seventh mission in the shuttle program. The space shuttle *Challenger* had made its first flight into space only two months earlier, in April 1983. It was the second of five shuttles that flew into space. A sixth shuttle was used as a test version and never flew in space.

THE *CHALLENGER* CREW

These were the people on board *Challenger* on Ride's first flight:

- Bob Crippen: The commander in charge of the mission
- Fred Hauck: The pilot, who helped the commander in controlling the craft
- Sally Ride, John Fabian, Norm Thagard: Mission specialists who performed scientific experiments, looked after the shuttle's cargo, and launched and captured satellites outside the craft.

The crew of STS-7 were (left to right): Sally Ride, Bob Crippen, Fred Hauck, Norm Thagard, and John Fabian.

WHAT WAS SPACE LIKE?

On Ride's first shuttle flight, *Challenger* zoomed through the clouds above Florida. The rocket boosters had fallen away into the ocean, but the orbiter was still fixed to the big fuel tank. The spacecraft was bursting through the edge of the atmosphere.

G-FORCE

Inside the cabin, Ride could hardly move. A massive force pressed her back in her seat. This was caused by **gravity**, but was much stronger. Because she was traveling so fast away from Earth, gravity's pull was increased. It reached three times (3 "G's") the normal force felt on the ground. Then, eight minutes after launch, the main engines stopped. The fuel tank was empty and dropped away. But the shuttle flew on, powered by its smaller engines. They were out of Earth's atmosphere.

The *Challenger* raced toward the edge of the atmosphere at 18,000 miles (28,000 kilometers) per hour.

SPACE Q AND A

Q. How does the shuttle keep moving?

A. Once the engines are off, you'd think the shuttle would slow down and stop. But this doesn't happen. Why not? Because in space there's no air, as there is in Earth's atmosphere, so there's nothing to "**drag**" on the craft and slow it down. It just keeps coasting along.

INTO ORBIT

Ride was suddenly flung forward as the feeling of **g-force** disappeared. Without the roar of the main engines, the ride was much smoother and quieter. The astronauts were in space at last.

The shuttle traveled on, up to a height of about 200 miles (322 kilometers). Here the pilot put the craft into orbit, so that it circled around Earth. All engines were shut off, and the only noise was the hum of the air conditioning.

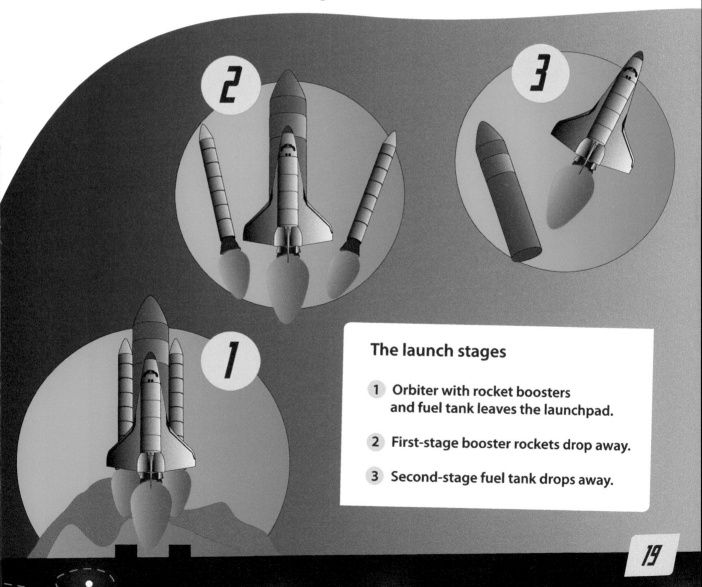

The launch stages

1. Orbiter with rocket boosters and fuel tank leaves the launchpad.

2. First-stage booster rockets drop away.

3. Second-stage fuel tank drops away.

LEARNING TO LIVE WITHOUT GRAVITY

"The best part of being in space is being weightless," Sally Ride wrote later. The first sign of this was when *Challenger* reached space and she saw that her papers and pencils were floating. In space, the effects of gravity are not felt because the spacecraft and crew are actually in free fall, constantly falling around and around Earth. Gravity is still present, but its effects are not felt.

People feel weightless, too. They simply float around inside the spacecraft. This means normal walking is impossible. Even the smallest movement can send you drifting through the air. To keep still, you have to grab hold of something that is fixed in place.

Ride and her crewmates had to learn a new way of moving around. The best way was to push off gently from a wall, then guide yourself with your hands through hatches and passages to where you wanted to be. The astronauts wore socks or slippers on board, in case they kicked someone by accident in mid-air.

On the flight deck, Sally Ride floated in the air while talking to ground control.

■ The astronauts are preparing a snack on board *Challenger*.

NO RIGHT WAY UP

If you are upside down on Earth, your blood and other **body fluids** will flow toward your head. The force of Earth's gravity is pulling it downward. But inside the shuttle, there was no up or down. Ride could lie on the floor or the ceiling or the walls without getting a headache—and without falling off.

Cleaning up

Weightlessness brings problems, too. Dust, food crumbs, and hairs float just like everything else. They easily drift into computers and air conditioning filters. This could cause damage, so every day the astronauts vacuum these areas to suck up the dirt.

DAILY LIFE IN SPACE

Astronauts have to do many of the same things we do on Earth. They eat, go to the bathroom, and sleep. But there is a big difference. They have to do all these things in weightless conditions.

Eating

Ride and the other crew members ate from trays strapped to their legs. Most of the food was sticky, so it stayed on the spoon. If it drifted off, it could make a terrible mess. But they had to keep hold of sandwiches. If they put them down, the slices would float apart!

Drinking

Ride couldn't drink from a glass. The liquid would not tip out without the effects of gravity. So she had to suck it out of a carton through a straw.

Going to the bathroom

Liquids would just float around in globules (balls of liquid). So, the astronauts were very careful not to make a mess in the toilet. Their body waste was sucked down a hose and into a tank below.

SPACE Q AND A

Q. What happens to your body in space?

A. Being weightless has some strange effects on a person:

• You get confused about up and down or right and left. This may cause dizziness and make you throw up.

• You grow taller. There is no weight on your spine, so it doesn't get compressed by gravity. Back on Earth, you'll "shrink" again.

• Your face becomes puffier. Your body fluids no longer drain downward, so more of them stay in your cheeks.

Sleeping

The crew members all slept at the same time. Some zipped themselves into sleeping bags, while others just floated asleep in mid-air. They wore black masks to keep out the sunlight.

Some astronauts strapped themselves to the walls of the spacecraft, to stop them from floating around when asleep.

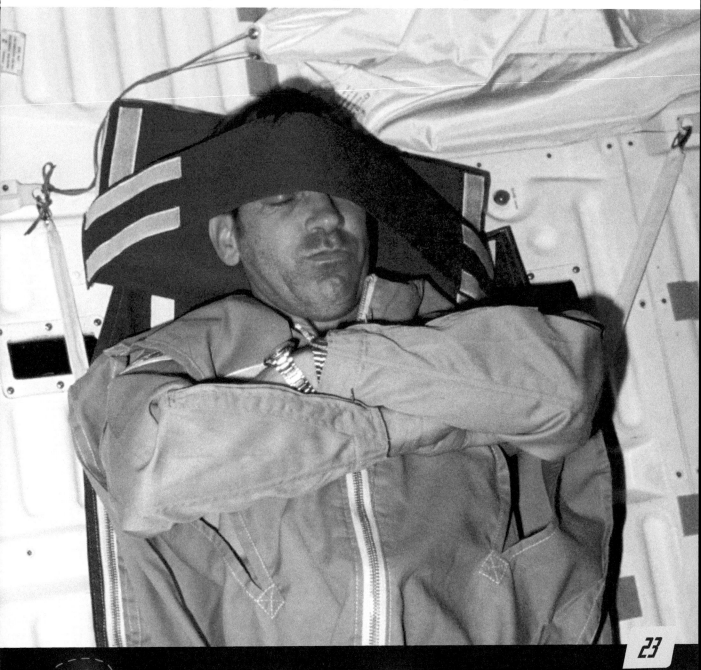

WORKING IN SPACE

One of the shuttle mission's main tasks was to launch new satellites into orbit. The satellites were carried up in the cargo bay. Launching was a complex process, and it required four of the crew members to work closely together. But it could be done from inside the spacecraft. Ride used her skills at operating the robot arm to lift the satellite out of the bay.

The shuttle's cargo bay was used to contain many items, including new satellites, spare parts, and tools.

WHAT ARE SATELLITES FOR?

A satellite is something that orbits another object in space. Human-made satellites come in all shapes and sizes. Some are as small as a soccer ball. Others are as big as a bus. They have many different uses:

- Weather satellites help us forecast what will happen with our weather.
- Observation satellites follow changes on Earth's surface.
- Broadcast satellites relay TV signals around the world.
- Navigation satellites help ships and aircraft to find their way.

OUT OF THE CARGO BAY

The satellite is placed on a small platform in the bay. It has to be launched at exactly the right moment, so that it heads in the correct direction of orbit. The crew inside sets the satellite spinning, then releases it. A system of springs sends it out of the bay. When it is safely away from the shuttle, rockets steer it into orbit.

SPACE Q AND A

Q. How do we launch satellites now?

A. The last shuttle mission was in 2011. Since then, every new satellite has been launched from Earth by rockets. The launch rocket flies to the edge of the atmosphere before turning into orbit. It then releases the satellite. The rocket burns up as it re-enters the atmosphere.

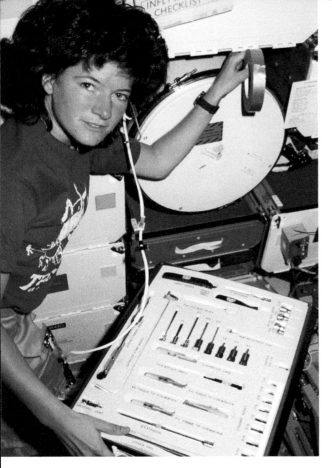

Ride shows some of the tools she needs for her work in space.

RESEARCH IN SPACE

The *Challenger* crew had another important role to play during their mission. They conducted several scientific experiments, exploring medical and technical processes. But why do these out in space? The answer is, because of weightlessness. They wanted to find out how the experiments were affected by weightless conditions.

ALLOYS, ANTS, AND ASTRONAUTS

Some of the experiments were set up in the cargo bay. One tested the making of metal alloys (mixtures of two or more metals) in space. Another studied a way of analyzing blood samples using electricity. Also in the bay was a colony of ants. Scientists wanted to know if they would behave differently when they were weightless.

The astronauts also ran tests on each other. They measured **blood pressure**, eye movement, and many other things. This helped scientists to understand how our bodies change during space flights.

LOOKING AT THE STARS

The shuttle carried powerful space telescopes. From Earth, our view of space is not completely clear. Moisture and dust in the atmosphere get in the way. But the shuttle was above the atmosphere, so its telescopes had a clear view of planets in the **solar system**, as well as distant stars and galaxies. The astronauts were able to gather detailed images and information about these objects, which they sent back to Earth.

Scientific experiments on board *Challenger* had to be checked regularly during the flight.

CATCHING SATELLITES

Another of the crew's tasks was to capture satellites already flying in space. Some satellites had been collecting information and had to be taken back down to Earth. Launching a satellite was hard enough. But recovering a satellite in orbit was much harder. First, they had to locate it as it circled Earth. Then, they had to fly the shuttle close to it when it passed by.

The "capture" was the job of the robot arm. Ride and another astronaut operated it from the flight deck inside the shuttle. They had to be careful to catch the satellite very gently with the grab at the end of the arm. A clumsy movement could damage the satellite. Once they'd captured it, they stored it in the cargo bay.

Even a big satellite is weightless in space. Three astronauts could easily lift and move it.

WORKING OUTSIDE

If a satellite needed repairs, two astronauts had to "**spacewalk**" (work outside the craft). They put on **space suits** and helmets with radios inside so they could speak to each other and the rest of the crew.

Once outside, they hooked their lines to the shuttle, to stop themselves from drifting off into space. Then they got to work on the satellite, using tools stored in the cargo bay. This sometimes took many hours.

This photograph shows the robotic arm on the shuttle *Colombia*. It is holding a satellite.

SPACE SPEAK

Space junk: Lower Earth Orbit is full of junk—and it is humans who put it there. Thousands of satellites circle Earth, together with bits of old spacecraft, fuel tanks, and spent rockets. NASA estimates that there are at least 20,000 pieces of space junk bigger than a tennis ball whizzing around the planet.

RETURNING TO EARTH

In the early morning of June 24, 1983, Ride and the crew were ready for the descent to Earth. Their mission in space had lasted six days—and they had traveled more than 2.5 million miles (4 million kilometers).

LEAVING SPACE

All five astronauts put on their launch and entry suits and were strapped into their seats. The pilot fired the engines to slow the shuttle's speed. This caused the craft to leave its orbit and fall back into Earth's atmosphere.

SPACE Q AND A

Q. What is it like to be on Earth again after a space flight?

A. Imagine you have been weightless for a week. Your body has been used to floating around. Your brain expects things to weigh very little. Your heart has been working less hard to pump your blood around. You've lost your sense of balance. How do you think you would feel as you climbed out of your spacecraft? For a start, you would find it hard to walk. Your legs would feel like lead, and it would take time to recover your sense of balance. Can you think of other problems?

SAFE LANDING

They were now moving fast. The air in the atmosphere dragged against the shuttle, creating intense heat. Through the window, Ride could see a bright orange glow around them. This would easily have melted the body of the craft. But it was protected by a layer of heat tiles glued to the outside. Then she saw the runway beneath them. The shuttle was gliding, with all engines off. The pilot guided it to land with a thump. They were home.

The astronauts were checked by a doctor before they could get off the shuttle.

BACK INTO ORBIT

As the first female American astronaut, Sally Ride was now a big celebrity. She was flooded with requests for interviews, photographs, and television appearances. But she wanted to get back to work. It was a relief when NASA gave her another space mission in late 1983.

Ride's second flight aboard *Challenger* was the 13th shuttle mission. It launched from Florida in the early morning of October 5, 1984. There were seven crew members on board, the most on any shuttle expedition.

Just nine hours after takeoff, Ride began using the robot arm to pick up and launch a new satellite. But there was a problem. The solar panels (which drew power from the Sun) got stuck. How could she fix this? Ride decided to give the satellite a good shake. She hadn't been trained to do this—but it worked!

Challenger's 1984 mission was the first to carry two women astronauts—Kathy Sullivan and Sally Ride.

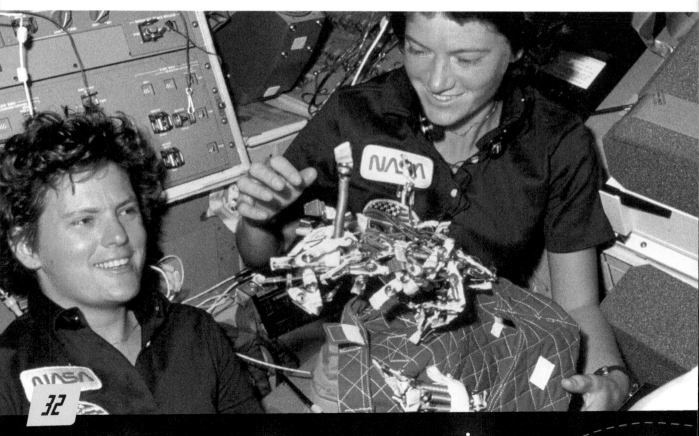

Once Ride was back on Earth, she made many television appearances, including on the children's television show "Sesame Street."

LANDMARKS

Over the next week, the *Challenger* crew completed many more tasks, including detailed photography of Earth and scientific experiments. This mission also saw some space "firsts." For the first time, two of the shuttle crew were women—Sally Ride and Kathy Sullivan. During the flight, Sullivan became the first American woman to spacewalk. Marc Garneau was the first Canadian to fly in space. Paul Scully-Power was the first Australian-born man in space. *Challenger* landed safely on October 13, after eight days in space.

Tricky touchdown

Landing was one of the most dangerous moments of a shuttle flight. The shuttle glided to Earth with no power, so the touchdown had to be perfect. As soon as the landing wheels hit the runway, a parachute opened on the tail and helped to brake the shuttle.

THE END OF *CHALLENGER*

In June 1985, NASA announced that Sally Ride would go to space again, a year later. But the mission never took place. Instead, the U.S. space program faced its biggest disaster yet.

On January 28, 1986, Ride was on her way to work in Texas. At the same time, far away in Florida, the *Challenger* was lifting off the launchpad. This was the 25th shuttle mission, and so far everything had gone perfectly.

Crowds on the ground watched the spacecraft roar upward, flames streaming behind it. Suddenly, the shuttle exploded and broke up. The flames became smoke trails as the different parts scattered across the sky. The seven members of the crew were all killed.

Just 73 seconds after takeoff, *Challenger* exploded, killing all on board.

WILLIAM ROGERS   SALLY RIDE

The special commission interviewed over 100 people during its investigation into the disaster.

FINDING OUT WHY

The tragedy shocked the world. Ride had been close friends with most of the *Challenger* crew. She knew it could just as easily have been her. The question was: Why did it happen?

Ride was part of the special **commission** that investigated the disaster. Its report showed that a **seal** on one of the rocket boosters had failed. This had allowed hot gas to escape and start a leak from the fuel tank. The result was a huge fire, which broke the craft apart.

The second shuttle tragedy

Space travel is very dangerous. The smallest fault can bring disaster. When the shuttle *Columbia* took off in January 2003, a piece of foam plastic broke off the fuel tank and hit the wing. This created a small hole. When the shuttle flew back into the atmosphere, this was enough to make it break apart. For the second time, an entire crew was lost.

WAS THE SPACE SHUTTLE PROGRAM IMPORTANT?

The shuttle program was shut down for two years after the *Challenger* disaster. Sally Ride never flew to space again. She retired from NASA in August 1987 and became a college professor. But, eventually, U.S. exploration of space continued—and so did the shuttle missions.

LOOKING INTO THE UNIVERSE

The program's most exciting achievements were still to come. Shuttle crews launched two **space probes** in 1989 to send back images of planets. The probe *Magellan* reached Venus in a year, while *Galileo* took nearly six years to reach Jupiter.

Then came the Hubble Space Telescope. The shuttle *Discovery* carried Hubble into Low Earth Orbit in 1990. Despite some early problems, the giant telescope has relayed more than a million amazing observations of distant planets, stars, and galaxies.

A NEW SPACE STATION

Finally, there was the building of a whole new space station. In 1998, shuttles were used to transport parts for the International Space Station (ISS). This flying research laboratory is made up of many **modules** (parts) that were fixed together in space. Without the shuttle fleet, it might never have been built.

Pictures from the Hubble Space Telescope (such as this shot of the Carina Nebula) have changed our ideas about outer space.

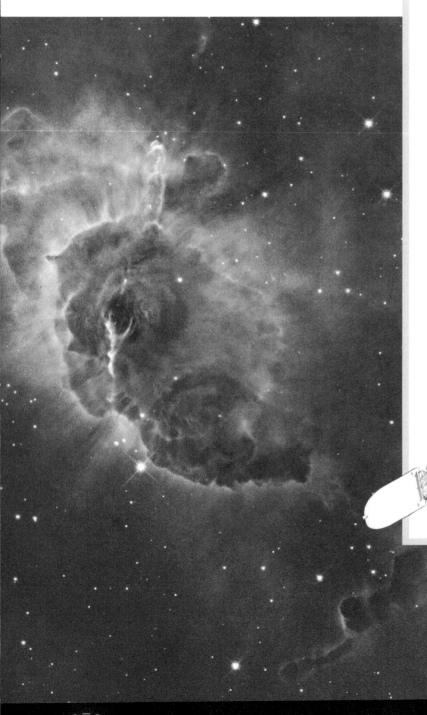

The best of Hubble

Here are some of the most astonishing things the Hubble Telescope has shown us:

- When the **comet** Shoemaker-Levy collided with Jupiter in 1994, Hubble gave us the best view.

- The universe is expanding, but data from Hubble showed that this expansion is getting faster.

- How old is the universe? Thanks to Hubble, scientists now think it is roughly 13.75 billion years old.

THE END OF THE SHUTTLES

The shuttles kept on flying for many years. Launched in 1981, the program was only meant to last for 100 missions. But then it was needed to build the ISS in 1998. After that, the life of these craft was extended several times.

It was not until 30 years after the first flight that the shuttles were retired from service. The final mission was number 135. It ended when *Atlantis* flew out of orbit and landed at the Kennedy Space Center, in Florida, on July 21, 2011.

The four surviving shuttle orbiters were transported to museums across the United States, where you can see them today.

- *Enterprise* is at the Intrepid Sea, Air, and Space Museum, in New York City.
- *Discovery* is at the Udvar-Hazy Center, in Chantilly, Virginia.
- *Atlantis* is at the Kennedy Space Center, in Merritt Island, Florida.
- *Endeavour* is at the California Science Center, in Los Angeles, California.

SPACE SHUTTLE-SUCCESS OR FAILURE?

The shuttles were some of the biggest and most complex machines ever built. They stayed in service for a long time and achieved many amazing things. Crews collected mountains of scientific data and launched satellites and space probes.

On the other hand, the shuttle program was very expensive. It cost almost $114 billion. It also cost the lives of 14 astronauts.

Space shuttle statistics

Number of shuttles built: 6 (though only 5 flew in space)

Total missions flown: 135

Total distance flown: 542 million miles (872 million kilometers)

Total time in space: 1,334 days (more than three and a half years)

Total number of astronauts: 355 (including 49 women)

Focus on:

FEMALE FIRSTS

More than 500 humans have flown in space. More than 50 of these have been women. Since Sally Ride's achievements in the 1980s, women have played a much bigger part in space exploration. Here are some of them:

ANNA LEE FISHER (UNITED STATES)

In 1983, Fisher gave birth to her first baby. Just over a year later, she went into orbit aboard the shuttle *Discovery*. She was the first mother in space.

HELEN SHARMAN (UNITED KINGDOM)

Helen Sharman was born in England. She worked as an engineer before being chosen to train at a Russian space school. In May 1991, she blasted off inside a **Soyuz** spacecraft. She was the first British woman in space.

■ Helen Sharman

MAE JEMISON (UNITED STATES)

After leaving Stanford University, Jemison worked as a volunteer doctor in refugee camps in Cambodia and West Africa. She then trained as an astronaut. In 1992, she became the first African American in space, flying on the shuttle *Endeavour*.

■ **Mae Jemison**

EILEEN COLLINS (UNITED STATES)

As a child, Collins loved watching aircraft taking off and landing. In 1990, she began training as a NASA astronaut, and she had her first space flight in 1995. Four years later, she became the first woman to command a shuttle mission.

LIU CHANG (CHINA)

Liu Yang's first ambition was to be a lawyer. But as an adult, she joined China's armed forces and became a skilled pilot instead. She was then selected to be an astronaut. In June 2012, she became the first Chinese woman to go into space.

WHAT NEXT?

Sally Ride was a great pioneer—not just as a woman in a profession usually led by men, but as an astronaut. She was also a great teacher. After leaving NASA, she started an education program to inspire young people with the wonders of science. The aim, she said, was "to make science cool." After a long and successful career, Ride died in 2012.

DREAM CHASER

Now that the space shuttles are gone, what will take their place? There is now only one way to get astronauts into Low Earth Orbit. This is aboard the Russian *Soyuz* spacecraft, but each flight costs the United States $70.7 million. One private company is developing the Dream Chaser for sending people into space. This will look like a much smaller version of the shuttle, but will still be capable of carrying seven astronauts up to the ISS.

NASA is also developing a new kind of orbiter for sending astronauts and supplies into deep space. They are likely to be very different from both the shuttle and the *Dream Chaser*.

The *Dream Chaser* is due to make its first test flight in November 2016.

■ Sally Ride believed passionately that children, especially girls, should be encouraged to reach their full potential.

A NEW SPACE RACE?

The first race into space was between two countries—the United States and Russia. Today, many other countries around the world are launching their own missions.

- China has already sent unmanned craft to the Moon. Now it plans to build a new space station.
- Japan aims to land a **humanoid robot** on the Moon.
- India and South Korea have sent rockets into orbit and plan to land on the Moon.
- Iran is developing a space program.

Meanwhile, what are the United States and Russia doing? The Russians are also aiming to land people on the Moon for the first time. But the Americans are looking to go much further—to land humans on **asteroids**, or even on Mars.

TIMELINE

May 26, 1951	Sally Ride is born in Los Angeles, California
July 20, 1969	*Apollo 11* lands the first humans on the Moon
August 12, 1977	First test flight of a space shuttle inside the atmosphere with astronauts on board
January 16, 1978	Ride is selected for NASA astronaut training
August 1979	Ride completes her training as a mission specialist
April 12, 1981	*Columbia* becomes the first shuttle to fly into space
June 18, 1983	Shuttle *Challenger* launches mission STS-7: Ride becomes the first American woman in space
October 5, 1984	Ride's second space mission (STS-41G) aboard *Challenger*
January 28, 1986	Shuttle *Challenger* breaks up on launch. Ride serves on the Rogers Commission, which investigates the disaster.
1987	Ride leaves the NASA astronaut corps
May 4, 1989	*Magellan* is the first deep space probe to be launched from a shuttle. Ride becomes director of the University of California's Space Institute.
April 24, 1990	Hubble Space Telescope is carried into space by a shuttle
December 4, 1998	Shuttles begin the construction of the International Space Station
April 1, 2003	Shuttle *Columbia* breaks up upon re-entry
July 21, 2011	*Atlantis* makes the last ever shuttle space flight
July 23, 2012	Sally Ride dies at the age of 61

GLOSSARY

air lock airtight chamber between two areas of unequal air pressure

asteroid rocky bodies of rock and iron that orbit the Sun

astronaut person trained to travel into space aboard a spacecraft

atmosphere protective layer of air and other gases that surrounds Earth, allowing living things to survive

blood pressure pressure of the blood in our bodies, pumped around by the heart

body fluids blood, water, and other liquids in our bodies

comet body that orbits the Sun; it is made up of a rock and ice, with a long tail of gas and dust

commission group of people that is appointed to study something or find out how a disaster occurred

drag force of the air in the atmosphere that holds back a flying object, such as a shuttle

g-force short for "gravity-force," a force of gravity, high loads of which are felt during rapid acceleration

glider winged aircraft without an engine

gravity pulling force that attracts objects to one another and prevents weightlessness

hatch opening or doorway in a spacecraft

humanoid robot robot that can be made to look and move like a human

Low Earth Orbit region between 100 and 1,240 miles (160 and 2,000 kilometers) above Earth's surface

module one of the living or working units that make up a spacecraft

orbit curved path an object follows around a planet, or other celestial body, as a result of its gravity

physics study of the science of matter (anything that occupies space) and energy

press conference interview given to news reporters and photographers by a famous person

psychiatrist doctor who studies people's personalities and, if necessary, treats their mental illnesses

rocket booster rockets used to help push space shuttles out of the pull of Earth's gravity

satellite object that orbits a star, planet, or asteroid. Satellites can be natural, such as the Moon, or human-made, such as *Sputnik 1*.

seal usually rubber that covers and closes a joint, or gap, between two parts of a machine

solar system Sun, with the eight planets, plus asteroids and other bodies, that orbit around it

Soyuz Russian spacecraft and launch system used to ferry crews to space stations

space probe unmanned craft sent to explore distant areas of space

space suit suit that protects astronauts from the hostile conditions in space (including very low pressure and lack of oxygen)

spacewalk go outside a spacecraft, usually to work on repairs to the spacecraft or a satellite

FIND OUT MORE

BOOKS

Bailey, Diane. *The Future of Space Exploration* (What's Next?). Mankato, MN.: Creative Education, 2013.

Goldsmith, Mike. *The Kingfisher Space Encyclopedia*. New York: Kingfisher, 2012.

Ride, Sally, with Susan Okie. *To Space and Back*. New York: Beech Tree, 1991.

Sparrow, Giles. *Space Exploration* (Space Travel Guides). Mankato, MN.: Smart Apple Media, 2012.

Stott, Carole. *Space Exploration* (Eyewitness). New York: Dorling Kindersley, 2014.

DVDS

The Dream Is Alive (1985)
Sally Ride is featured in this short history of space shuttle flights.

Story of the Space Shuttle (2012)
This is a documentary history of the shuttle program.

WEB SITES

Facthound offers a safe, fun way to find Internet sites related to this book. All of the sites on Facthound have been researched by our staff.

Here's all you do:
Visit www.facthound.com
Type in this code: 9781484625163

HOW CAN I FIND OUT MORE?

The shuttle missions are now part of history. But the human exploration of space is still going on. Here are some ideas for you to research:

- Space tourism: Would you like to go "on vacation" to space? Some people have already! How much would it cost and how dangerous would it be?

- The Hubble Space Telescope: How does the HST work? There are many sites about the telescope and the amazing photographs it has taken of deep space.

- Flying to Mars: Mars is over 140 million miles (225 million kilometers) away. Will humans ever land on the Red Planet? Find out more about our nearest neighbor and how we might get there.

- Was the space shuttle program worthwhile? Do you think it was worth the huge amount of money and the lives of 14 people? What were the positive results? Start your research by looking up "How much does a shuttle cost?" in the Frequently Asked Questions section of the NASA web site.

INDEX